CW00663033

CHAPTER 1: THE BEGINNING OF MY DECENT

It started when I was 17 years old. Certain, events, happened that forced me into a situation I never thought I would be in. Ever since I was 8, I have considered myself an Atheist. Even before that I was never truly convinced by religion, I just never knew there was another option other than believing in "God."

Now.. After putting all of my thoughts into this book, I'm no longer sure what to believe.. I've only ever believed in what the facts could prove, but now all the facts are pointing to the one thing that can't be true..

Am I losing my mind?

I can't be the..

I'm in a situation where I feel I am either on the brink of something great, but with what that could mean, it may be best to burn this and leave it in my past..

Can I escape destiny?

Or am I trapped in fate?*

Science has intrigued, disappointed, and infuriated me ever since I was young.

With Science, we have proven we are capable of anything, only limited by the resources at our disposal. We have made this world far better than it was in only a few short centuries. We have also shown we are capable of destroying it in only a few short moments.

Religion has intrigued, disappointed, and infuriated me ever since I was young.

With Religion, we have proven we are capable of incredible feats, only limited by our own beliefs. On one side, we have tried to mold our world into a peaceful society. On the other, we have shown we are willing to destroy any force that may oppose our beliefs.

For a while, I believed that Science rendered religion pointless, almost redundant. That was until I began seeing connections between all of the diverse religions. This is when I began thinking of many different possible theories. Perhaps they were more than just stories we made up to try and understand what was at the time, impossible for us to comprehend. Instead I looked at each as individual pieces to a puzzle.

All that follows are my attempts of putting the pieces together. I must warn you, what you are about to read will contradict many beliefs in both the field of Religion and Science. I will purposely contradict many of my own interpretations throughout this book because I feel it is important to explore all possibilities to find the truth.

CHAPTER 2: GENESIS, OR SO TO SPEAK

Scientists have dated the start of the Universe(s) farther back than a 14 billion years. The process they used to determine this is actually quite simple.

Using the Big Bang theory which simply states that in beginning there was nothing until the universe exploded and began expanding outwards. They have observed that objects in space are constantly drifting apart from each other.

To figure how old the Universe(s) may be, they took the current distance between galaxies and the rate at which they are drifting apart, and simply worked backwards.

To suggest that this is an accurate equation is not something any Scientist can answer honestly, but it is the closest we can get given our current knowledge of the Universe(s).

By studying the Universe(s), they have discovered it takes millions of years for light from distant galaxies to reach us. So by the time the light reaches us, the formations we think we see beginning to form may already have completely formed or even have reached the end of their life cycle.

This contradicts many different religions who accept that God created the Universe(s) and everything in it in only a week. This is a belief perhaps most famously shared between Judaism, Islam, and Christianity. Given what we now know, it is reasonable to assume this belief is not a fact.

Scientists have dated human life farther back than 100,000 B.C. Due to Archeological findings, they have found a substantial amount of evidence to support the Theory of Evolution. Basically, the Theory of Evolution states that all organic life started out as single cell organisms gradually evolving into more complex creatures through a series of mutation and natural selection.

To simplify, if you look at the remains of a human dated 50,000 years ago and compare it to the remains of a human dated 5,000 years ago, you will find a significant difference not only in the physical appearance of their bone structure, but you would also see their tools were more, sophisticated.

Many people would argue that this proves that life was not created by a divine being, that we are nothing but a cosmic accident. I too would have argued this until I stopped and considered that they may both be right in their own ways.

Arguing on side with divine creation, I say take a look at anything we have ever created. We are constantly improving upon the original model making each one surpass the last. If you consider us as nothing more than "models," I feel it would be reasonable to assume any divine creator would improve on his creations in the same way.

There is an idea we are all created from dust. At first I thought this was absurd.

That was until Scientists discovered we are essentially created out of Star-dust. They found Star-dust is the key component for all organic and non-organic materials throughout the universe. So I decided perhaps the fallacy was due to poor translation.

Even more startling is when I looked at the word Soul. We believe our soul is basically our energy/life force. I then compared it to the word Sol. Sol is defined as Sun or light. Given the similarity between the two words and their definition, I felt this may back up the idea that our soul is the concentration of Star-dust.

If this is all true, could this be the missing link in our understanding of just what consciousness is? We have always assumed the two were connected but given the friction between Science and Religion we decided that there must be another explanation.

CHAPTER 3: JOURNEY OF THE SOUL

I would argue the most influential part of all religions spanning from ancient mythology to modern theistic beliefs, is the Afterlife. It is said that humans have always believed in a life after death. Archeological findings have determined we may have always buried our dead which initially led to this belief.

For the sake of argument, let's look at the alternative. If we hadn't buried our dead they would have been left to decompose and rot. Burying them would have been done out of necessity after that.

You could then argue the fact that the dead were buried with their belongings could indicate we believed they would have use for them in the Afterlife.

Again, let's look at the alternative.

If they weren't buried along-side them, and considering our nature to take things that we want, I would assume there were many fights perhaps even deaths due to the fact the belongings of the deceased could now belong to anybody. Burying their belongings would be the smartest solution.

I feel our belief in an Afterlife could possibly be due to our uncontrollable desire to live forever. Perhaps this is due to a strong survival instinct or fear that we really are insignificant in the grand plan of the Universe(s). Maybe given the strong connection we build with each other while we are alive, the Afterlife could simply be a tool to cope with the loss of a loved one.

Accepted throughout a majority of religions, there are two separate places that make up the Afterlife. One is the place where good people go commonly referred to as Heaven, or Paradise. The other is the place where the evil people are sent commonly referred to as Hell, or the Underworld.

Throughout these religions there have been a set of guidelines to follow that determine which one your soul will go to. The most prevalent of these guidelines are do not kill your fellow man, and worship your God(s). Unfortunately when there are more than one God(s) humans murder one another because we feel the latter of the two is more important.

*If I accomplish anything out of this, I hope to bring an end to the unnecessary conflict brought on by mere misconceptions. *

Given our actions are driven by a desire to enter Heaven, just take a minute and really think about Heaven and what it would take to truly be considered a Paradise. I have heard many different ideas of what Heaven would be like so I will go through and break them down.

One idea is that you will receive your own piece of Heaven where you will have everything you could ever possibly want. A more accepted idea is that Heaven is one grand community where the streets are paved with gold and everyone is happy.

What if everyone you ever cared for wasn't allowed in and were sent to Hell? Would Paradise really be Paradise to you knowing that?

My opinion may very well change when I'm faced with the end, but for right now I am comfortable with the idea that in the end, you enter an endless sleep. Everything just shuts off and you're left with nothing but silent darkness.

Another common belief is Reincarnation, which is believed to have started as early as early-Greece and is now most predominant in Indian cultures. Reincarnation is a belief that when you die your soul will be reborn again into another creature. The people who follow this believe their actions in this life determine the creature they will return as.

The common interpretation is if you were to live your life doing good deeds you will return as something majestic like a bird or lion. If you live your life doing evil deeds, you will return as something graceless like a slug or roach. Some even believe you could be reincarnated as another human given certain circumstances and/or if you are given permission by your God(s).

As things stand right now, no-one can truly claim that there is an Afterlife. Even if a person was to die and come back, their claims really hold no truth since it is hard to determine if their mind simply played tricks on them.

Science has shown us that when any living creature dies, energy is released and is essentially absorbed by the earth during the processes of decomposition.

Assuming the energy released is the living creature's soul, Reincarnation would be the most reasonable belief since there energy will be distributed into another living creature through the energy cycle.

A simplified version of the energy cycle states that the Sun gives energy to the grass, which in turn gives energy to the cow, which then gives its energy to the human. Then assuming God(s) did have a hand in the creation, could they simply be recycling energy? That might be an oversimplification but it would be plausible in this consensus.

CHAPTER 4: GODS AND TITANS

Perhaps the thing that confused me most when I was young was how used to have a widespread belief in a multiple Gods then seemingly out of nowhere it is now accepted there is only one true God.

I constantly wondered what could have happened to change us from a polytheistic society to a strictly mono-theistic society. Then I, "humanized," the God(s) and considered again that maybe everyone only had different pieces of a puzzle.

*As I begin to explain myself throughout these pages, note that I will be focusing a great deal on Greek mythology. The reason for this being that I feel it provides the best background for bringing everything together. I am considering all religions are one in the same, the only difference being that the Gods were given different aliases and perhaps roles based on the culture of the people who worshipped them. To start, I will begin in the beginning. *

The Greeks believed that in the beginning there was nothing but chaos. Then out of the chaos, love emerged.

*Looking at what we now know they just described the time right after the Big Bang. In fact, every single ancient mythology have some form on the Big Bang in their beliefs. The Greeks definition for Love may be the force we now describe as Gravity. Gravity as far as we know is the force that pushes and forms everything in existence. It is the force the keep you on the ground and keeps you from floating into space. *

They believed the first "beings" were Ouranus and his wife Gaia. Some teaching actually depicted them as the embodiments of chaos and love. Ouranus was known as the father of the Universe and Gaia as the mother of Earth. Some scholars believe that when any belief system references to the Universe and Earth, they actually refer to the two as space and matter respectively.

Ouranus and Gaia had many children together, among these were hundred handed giants known as Hecatoncheires, 3 Cyclops', and 12 Titans.

The Titans were known as Cronus, Oceanus, Iapetus, Hyperion, Clymene, Coes, Rhea, Tethys, Theia, Phoebe, Themis, and Mnemosyne.

It is said Gaia gave control of seven planetary systems over to the Titans. It is not known how they divided the control between them but as far as we know they lived peacefully amongst each other having many children between themselves. Most notable in mythology were Atlas and Prometheus, brothers born from Iapetus and Clymene.

Their Father, Ouranus feared that his children would one day overthrow him so he took his children and grandchildren and threw them into a bottomless pit known as Tartarus.

Cronus, the eldest Titan, escaped his father's wrath and with his mother, Gaia, plotted revenge against him. Gaia made Cronus a sickle and told Cronus to ambush his father while he slept. Following his mother's orders, Cronus ambushed his father, castrated him and threw his genitals into the sea.

It is said Aphrodite emerged from the seed that fell into the sea, and Giants were born from the ichor, or blood that fell on the land.

Beaten, Ouranus retreated. His final words to his son were that someday his children would betray him just as he had betrayed him.

Cronus now controlled the Universe(s) and with his wife, Rhea, gave birth to the beings we now call "the Olympic Gods."

These Gods are known as Hestia, Demeter, Hera, Hades, Poseidon, and Zeus. To prevent his father's prophecy from coming true, Cronus ate his children as soon as they were born.

All except for the youngest, Zeus.

Rhea tricked Cronus by giving him a stone to swallow and then hid Zeus away from him. It is said his grandmother Gaia, harbored him until he was ready to take on his father. When he was fully mature, he confronted his father and during the fight, he vomited the swallowed Gods and they aided Zeus in his fight.

When they had won, they threw Cronus into Tartarus and Zeus claimed control of the throne. Now, drunk with power, he went to war with the remaining Titans and all that would threaten his power.

Some of the Titans sided with Zeus and helped him fight in what could only be described as a cataclysmic battle. Among these Titans was Prometheus who would later play a major role.

Nothing this massive had ever taken place before and in the end, Zeus, with his army, had won. Some of his enemies were simply thrown into Tartarus while others he chose special punishments. Prometheus' brother, Atlas, was forced to hold the weight of the heavens on his shoulders for all eternity. Thus began the rule of the Olympic Gods as we know today.

CHAPTER 5: THE NINE WORLDS

Expanding now to Norse mythology. The followers of this religion believed in nine different worlds all connected by the World Tree. Each world was inter- connected by a series of branches.

The Egyptians shared a similar belief. They believed that when the universe(s) was given order it took the form of a Great ocean expanding and breaking into many different streams. This belief is even supported to some degree by Scientists today. Scientists believe that there may indeed be multiple Universe(s) that would have to be connected by some fabric of space.

In comparing the Greeks belief in "seven planetary systems" with the Nordic belief in nine worlds, I found there may indeed be similarities between the two.

One of the nine worlds is known as Asgard. Asgard is known as the kingdom where most gods live which could be depicted as Ouranus' kingdom until Cronus took over. So given this it couldn't be one of the seven given to the Titans. It is also thought to be where Valhalla is located. Valhalla is believed to be where the heroic are sent as a reward for their heroism.

Only six were depicted as being habited my mortals. These are Vanahain, Alfhaim, Svartalfaim, Midgard (Earth), Jofunheim, and Nidavellir.

The eighth world is known as Helheim and its counterpart Niflheim. Heliheim was the realm were the common dead would go who were neither evil nor heroic. Niflheim was the realm where the truly evil were sent.

The ninth world is Muspelheim. Muspelheim is depicted as a "chaotic" world ruled by a powerful "demon." This may be there interpretation of Tartarus and the powerful "demon" may be a reference to Cronus. Although Tartarus has generally always been depicted as being a part of Earth. If that is the case, perhaps a more plausible explanation would be it is the realm where Ouranus retreated to since he was once referred to as the embodiment of chaos.

With either explanation, the seven planetary systems could be Vanahaim, Alfhaim, Svartalfaim, Midgard, Jotunheim, Nidvallir, and Helheim. These worlds were even given detailed descriptions.

Vanahaim, is known as the home of the Vanir. Vanir were depicted as being "god-like" in terms of stature. The Vanir were thought to focus mainly on agriculture. This world is said to have four perfect seasons and a significantly longer year than ours.

Alfaim is known as the home of Elves. Elves are depicted as being demi-god like creatures more luminous than the sun. Could they be Angles as we have come to think of in modern theology?

Svartalfaim, is known as the realm of the Dark Elves. It is said to be a dark and inhospitable realm. The atmosphere is thought to be dark and miserable. Could the dark elves be the Angles that have been come to know as the Fallen Angels?

Jotunheim, is known to be the home of the Giants. It's depicted as being a largely forested realm surrounding a civilization, similar to that found in Midgard.

Nidvallir, is known as the home of the dwarves. They were depicted as excellent blacksmiths. The realm of Nidvallir is thought to be mountainous realm filled with mines and the inhabitants are thought to live in underground societies.

Would this mean we were in fact told about life on other planets? Whether we were or not, we can't deny it would be nothing short of ignorant if we truly believed that we were the only life in the vastness of the Universe(s).

CHAPTER 6: PROMETHEUS THE CREATOR OF MAN

If you have made it this far, I can only apologize for what comes next. I will be conflicting with many, if not all beliefs we have from here on out. I will be connecting mythology and modern theism using scriptures that have been discovered but rejected from teachings due to conflicting messages. This new understanding could hold the key to understanding the truth to everything. I don't want to come across as if I think I have all the answers. The worst thing I could do right now is to claim that I do, but if any of this makes any sense, or even expands your mind, then that should mean something.

In Greek mythology, Prometheus is known as the creator of man. It is not fully explained how he came up with the idea for man, all that is said is that our purpose was to worship the Gods.

Something about our prayers apparently made the Gods more powerful. If I was to even begin to explain this in a dare I say, scientific way, perhaps once again assuming that our soul is the concentration of star-dust, maybe there is a reaction from our prayer that releases energy that causes them to gain power through some sort of symbiotic relationship we share with each other?

I think the biggest problem we have in the way we perceive Gods and Goddesses is we see them as omnipotent beings that are capable of working outside the realm of physics and can bend reality to their will.

What if they are confined to the same reality as us but simply have a better understanding? My point being take a look at what we now know about Earth and how we fit into it.

Only a very small portion is actually inhabitable for human life. Even so we are still in danger of natural disasters such hurricanes, volcanic eruptions, earthquakes, severe droughts, etc.

Assuming once again that we were created by a divine being, I feel it would be reasonable to claim the Earth wasn't really made for us, rather it was a suitable place for us to live.

We know that Dinosaurs roamed this planet far before humans. It's accepted that a cataclysmic event occurred that wiped all of them out. One theory is a meteorite crashed down creating a series of events that killed them all off but perhaps it was something else entirely.

We have determined it's very likely that at one point all of the Earths land was one land mass and over time they drifted apart through an event we call Pangea. Giving what we have observed in the formation of planets, we know that at one point we did not have a moon. Even more peculiar, we now believe we may have had two moons at one point.

Given what we know about moons, they are nothing more than an asteroid or combination of objects that get caught in a planets gravitational pull and/or form into what we know today.

We have discovered that moons seem to stabilize the planets they orbit. It has been determined that if our moon had not been caught in our orbit, life on our planet would be much different due to the fact our seasons would be more intense and far longer.

If I tried to explain this in a way including divine intervention, it would seem that the moon was placed so that humans would be able to survive. If there were really two separate moons, perhaps the extra gravitational pull contributed to Pangea pulling the continents apart in a tug-o-war fashion.

We believe that the two moons could have possibly fused together into the moon we now see today. Evidence for this is a significant difference in characteristics on the side visible to us and the side hidden.

Sorry, got a little side tracked.

Prometheus is depicted as a compassionate being towards man. He is known by the Greeks as the one that brought us fire. Consider perhaps that they didn't consider fire to be an object, but perhaps more likely what it is; a chemical reaction. They could possibly mean that he exposed us to Science.

As the story goes, Zeus didn't want us to have "fire" so when Prometheus betrayed him, Zeus punished him by chaining him to a mountain where an eagle came every day to eat his liver. His liver would then rejuvenate overnight and the eagle would return the next day to repeat his punishment.

You will find a similar teaching in a rejected scripture depicting the story of Adam and Eve. In this scripture the serpent is depicted as being a hero for exposing man to fruit of knowledge. Could this mean the "devil" we have come to hate could possibly be our creator?

To support this theory, another version of the story claims Adams' first wife was a women named Lilith. As this story goes, they were both equals but Adam wanted her to be subordinate and because of this, she left him. She was then depicted as rebelling against her creator because she felt betrayed and she was the known for being the source of the first sin.

Could this mean we really are only stuck in a power struggle between our creator and his king?

*I warned you. It's not too late to stop. *

CHAPTER 7: ZEUS AND HIS ARMY OF ANGELS

The Greeks only really focused on the Olympians and there interactions with our planetary systems. We know that during the War against the Titans that some of the Titans and their children joined Zeus so it would be safe to assume they were left to occupy the remaining ones and the Olympians took dominion over Ouranus kingdom and dubbed it Olympus.

Given the Nordic belief in multiple worlds, perhaps the remaining Titans and their children settled in these worlds.

If this is true, perhaps upon Prometheus' invention of Man and what that would mean towards power, they created their own versions of Man so that Prometheus and/or the Olympic Gods didn't become even more powerful than them. If this became an "arms race" so to speak, this could take the randomness out of Evolution. Perhaps, making a "perfect" being is difficult for any creator.

Given his nature, Zeus would not have accepted any chance of him losing control over his kingdom. Would it be reasonable to assume that he might feel he needed to build an army? Hephaestus is known as the blacksmith of the Gods. It would make since if he went to Hephaestus and ordered him to build him an army and virtually indestructible soldiers that would obey only him. Thus, perhaps the Angels were created. They are normally depicted as being powerful soldiers of God, so this could make this theory plausible.

One of the rejected scriptures known as the book of Enoch talks about the time before the Great Flood. It claims that God sent down Angels and they begin to have relations with the women and creating offspring called Nephilim, which were depicted as terrible monsters that endangered all of Man.

It claims the flood was actually an attempt to destroy the Nephilim along with the evil among man. If this was in fact true, this could have been a tactic to force Prometheus into submitting a larger claim of his "share" of man into Zeus' control.

Which could lead us to the creation of our poly-theistic religions starting in Egypt and Sumerian settlements depending on when the flood actually took place. The story of Moses may be exposed to a different light.

What if Zeus punished Prometheus sometime after the flood? If you consider the fact that the Hebrew people have always believed in one supreme creator this could be interpreted as they have always worshiped Prometheus. What if he wasn't the one that led the Hebrews on the path that led them to being enslaved to further assert his dominance? What if it was Zeus?

When Moses spoke to God on the mountain, perhaps the reference to the burning bush could be a reference to Prometheus since he is known as the fire bringer. The Plagues set upon Egypt may suggest that Prometheus was aided by Apollo who was known as the God of Pestilence or disease, and perhaps even Hades and his wife Demeter who were known as the God of Death and Harvest including Famine who were crucial aspects of the plagues as well. Although I will admit I may just be trying to force these pieces together.

Regardless, it is said Moses succeeded in freeing the Hebrews. After suffering this defeat, I would assume that Zeus would need to act to save face.

This is when I presume Zeus set out to gain total control using his army to wipe out all of the Gods. Then using his army of Angels, he sent them to tell all of Man throughout the worlds of his supreme rule. Since the Gods seem to be immortal beings, I can only assume he put them into Tartarus, which is still depicted in some sacred texts used in modern theism today.

Hephaestus was known as a trickster. It is accepted across every religion that a group of Angels rebelled against him. Given these facts perhaps the Angels that rebelled were given free will and tried to stop Zeus' tyranny but failed and were cast out and were then depicted as being evil.

Given this, look at the story of Jesus Christ that Christians have based their faith off of. Many different versions of his story have been told dating all the back to the Egyptian god Horus. Both were born of a virgin, delivered a message from their father, both of who are considered to be the most powerful of the Gods, and were then crucified to ascend and become a God of their own.

It would stand to reason that since the Jews were still worshipping Prometheus, and the Romans had adopted the Greeks religion after conquering them, Jesus was sent to potentially convert them into worshipping Zeus, who may have been his father, with the promise of Paradise.

This would make more since of his strange behaviors especially towards the end. It is said he was tempted by the devil three times in the desert. Could this have been the Fallen Angels trying to explain what was really happening?

Would that make sense of when he told his followers he wasn't sent to bring peace but to wield a sword? Could his attempt in trying to show he was the messiah depicted in the Hebrew Scriptures toward the end of his life, be a way of going against his Father Zeus when he realized the truth? If Jesus did ascend, which side would he be on?

I'm sorry.

CHAPTER 8: CONNECTING THE DOTS IN REVELATIONS

There are many references to mythological beliefs in Revelations. Be it cross species animals which are predominant in Greek and Egyptian mythology, or the many headed serpent which could be interpreted as a Hydra.

Then there are the Four Horseman. War, Pestilence, Famine, and Death which are said to come out of the bottomless pit. War can be interpreted as being Ares, Zeus son and God of War. Famine can be interpreted as Demeter, Zeus sister God of the Harvest. Death can be interpreted as Hades, Zeus brother God of the Underworld. Pestilence, I feel I should mentioned has also been named Conquer. This Horseman is said to carry a bow. The bow was said to be Apollo's symbol and as I mentioned earlier, he is also known as the God of Pestilence.

Could that again mean that the dragon we think may be the Devil, actually refer to Prometheus?

Many people accept the fact that The Apocalypse refers to the end of days. This is what makes what I'm doing right now potentially very dangerous. Whether any of this is based in reality, I am by the literal definition; the False Prophet.

I am doing because I want to save the world from itself; the False Prophet will appear as the Lamb. I am writing this in a book I want to publish to potentially make a substantial profit off of; the False Prophet will attempt to profit off of his word. I can't even say I honestly believe any of this; the False Prophet will not believe his word. The fact that this makes sense is the most troubling; the False Prophet will speak words that seem true.

It is said the False Prophet will reveal the identity of the Anti-Christ. Would this be one of our fellow man? One of the Fallen? Or is the Anti-Christ as we have come to believe really Prometheus coming to wage war against Zeus?

Of course, above all else the job of the False Prophet is to set up a False Idol for worship and lead you astray.

Many feel the Whore of Babylon is a woman come forth as another sign for the end of days. Some scholars feel this might be interpreted as an unholy union of cities. The whore is said to sit on seven mountains. Seven is usually used throughout most sacred texts as a sign of completion. The word mountain is said to mean multiple things.

What if the mountains mean the seven continents of the world? Although we now consider there to only be six since Europe and Asia are one land mass. Ignoring technicalities, if the number seven is being used at a synonym for completion, then could the Whore of Babylon mean the unholy union of all cities?

Would that make the duty of the False Prophet to unite the world under a single banner so to speak?

If you consider the fact that Revelations was written in Greek, it changes the entire concept of the book. Apokálypsis, the Greek word for Apocalypse, has an entirely different meaning. This version of the word simply means an "unveiling." Could this possibly mean that the False Prophets job is to in fact change the world by exposing man to the truth?

Even more peculiar is the number 666 as we believe to be the mark of the beast written in Greek is the same as "in the name of Allah (God)" in Islamic calligraphy. Could this again suggest that the beast is the God that is worshipped in Judaism and Islamic theism? Would this in fact mean that Jesus is evil since he is depicted as bringing an end to the world or perhaps his second coming could mean something else entirely.

Given what we know about the Universe(s), and at least considering the "Gods" do have to work in the confines of reality that perhaps they only have a deeper understanding of Science. Would they really destroy one of the potentially few planets that can sustain there "perfect" creation?

The Atheist in me is telling me I'm wrong. The Philosopher in me wonders what if I'm right. Am I dealing with a Messiah Complex? Or..

CHAPTER 9: CAN THE TRUTH BE FOUND IN SCIENCE FICTION?

If you didn't think I was insane, you may begin to now. All that follows may contradict everything up to this point, or possibly confirm it.

It is nearly impossible to deny the human race has in fact been touched by Extra-Terrestrial life. There have been countless documentations of alien life making contact with us throughout the history dated back to ancient times. This may be an insignificant detail but by definition, the Gods we worship are alien life forms.

What if the Gods as we have come to know are simply our misconception for a greatly superior species? Think about this for a second. Our species has had a tendency to view things to be far superior than they truly are. If some being was to come down and perform extraordinary tasks, would we not view them as God-like?

Scientists have found an undefinable component in DNA that cannot be found in anywhere else on Earth. This brought on the idea that the meteorite that wiped out the dinosaur, brought the organisms that man evolved from.

The discoveries we have made today suggest that if Alien life did in fact contact us, they have been aiding us in our survival. Some evidence even suggest they exposed us to the concept of science. Could they in fact be the beings we know as the Serpent of Eden or Prometheus?

If we are willing to truly accept the fact that there is life throughout the Universe(s), would it be too hard to conceive we have already been in contact? Could these pieces I have been putting together be nothing more than a puzzle they left for us to piece together when we were ready to ascend to the next level of our intelligence? Would that make sense of this conflict between the Gods? Are they simply fighting for control over us or even our planet?

Many more questions surround this theory than I would like there to be but this is as much of a viable option as any other.

If they do have a hand in our evolutionary process, could this be my purpose? To "unveil" that they are nothing more than a superior humanoid not the Gods we have come to believe in?
Have I lost all credibility for exploring this option?
Or is the information we need to further advance our intellect?

Let's explore an alternative, perhaps these Aliens are the Angels. If you compare interactions with the two they are almost similar experiences. Most people who claim to have seen either the Angels or Aliens will say they are surrounded in a bright light. In ancient times, Aliens were depicted as bringing forth information and destruction to man similar to the Angels. Could the Gods we know merely be some form of their alien Hierarchy on distant planet?

Today, when you hear about alien abductees you consider it to be a made up story. Alien conspiracies are one of the most controversial topics we have today due to the fact that any evidence we may have is discredited as a hoax. If aliens are truly abducting us to perform experiments on us, are they searching for something? Someone?

..Me?

The far more likely explanation if they truly made contact, they tried to explain the Universe to us. If you look at the roles that we gave the Gods you would see they seemingly are nothing more than physical embodiments used to make the teaching of the cosmic forces easier. Could they truly have been nothing more than visual aids installed to aid us on all of our discoveries and just blown out of proportion?

Could this mean that to enter the next stage of intelligence we are supposed to abandon our beliefs? Is religion nothing more than an invention we made up? Could the Prophets as we come to believe been set on their path by an alien race? Believe it or not this has been theorized by many people since there is a substantial amount of evidence to this claim.

The Indian god Krishna is depicted as having blue skin and having access to advanced weaponry. Some scholars believe that this was merely to signify his divinity while others believe he could have indeed been sent by a foreign species.

There has even been paintings of Jesus Christ's conception, baptism and of his crucifixion that all have a clear depiction of UFOs in the sky above him shining a light on the scene. Of course the people who painted them weren't actually at these events so they hold no real credible evidence but some theories have even gone as far to say he and Krishna were a cross species between man and alien. This is not an entirely Ludacris idea given the circumstances.

Modern alien conspiracies as we have come to known seem to all have originated from Roswell, New Mexico where it is said an alien spacecraft crash landed. This led to the belief the government has a secret base where they either house or experiment alien life in a place called Area 51 and many more all around the world.

The prophet Muhammad is believed to have ascended to the moon on a winged horse and split it in two. We know that he didn't in fact split the moon in two. Perhaps the ascension of the Prophet Muhammad could have been an abduction? The second moon could be a misinterpretation of a UFO. To further support this theory is that in many depictions of the Gods throughout our history have been depicted as coming down in winged chariots, dragons, even clear descriptions of what we know as flying saucers. With this information, the winged horse might have even been a reference to this.

Which is more likely. A Pegasus, or winged horse prevalent in ancient Greek mythology, was on our Earth a little over 1000 years as it is believed to be when the prophet Muhammad had lived. Or an alien species came to abduct him.

There have been countless theories the aliens live on our very moon, ranging from images depicting UFOs flying across the surface to what appears to be bases built on the on the side not exposed to us. Many of these have come directly from ex-astronauts although it is hard to give these claims any credibility.

There are clear depictions of what could be depicted as ETs carved into walls in the tombs and temples on nearly every single continent spread throughout the world. Civilizations that are believed to have never come in contact with each other share similar depictions spread throughout our timeline.

These depictions all tend to show a short humanoid with a round head coming out of the saucers from the sky and some of them have what seem to be a depiction of what looks like a light bulb of sorts which as we know they would not have had any knowledge of. They have been described as lizard people, to ant men, and even a modern representation as being called grey men.

As crazy as all of the conspiracy theories may seem to the general public, if you were to weigh the evidence we have supporting an alien race versus the evidence we have supporting a divine creator, the evidence for the alien race greatly outweighs the divine creator.

Could religion be nothing more than a test set by them to see if we can overcome blind faith and replace it with reason? Could they even be as lost as we are in discovering their origins?

In ancient Indian texts, it's said at one point three giant cities of the Gods were orbiting the Earth. They were described as being made of gleaming metal and at one point the giant cities went to war with each other, destroying ancient cities in the cross-fire. It is said that the people who survived the battles, were then afflicted with boil like growths on their bodies and a having a loss in their hair and fingernails. This is a common effect of radiation poisoning as we know today with our use in nuclear weaponry.

Similar accounts can be described in the bible with the story of Sodom and Gomorrah. It is said God sent for his Angels to destroy the two cities for the sin of man, but what if this event was turned into a story as to force us to cower under the power of these "Angels"?

In the rejected book of Enoch, there is another telling of the story we know was Noah's Ark. In the scrolls it tells of Noah's immaculate-conception. This was probably rejected from religious text because it might've conflicted with the story of Jesus being the one true son of God.

Apparently Noah's mother became pregnant while his father was away. She claimed she had not been with another man and she had no idea how she had become with child.

Convinced she was lying Noah's father went to get advice from his own father. His father didn't offer any advice because he believed his wife had not committed adultery so he then went to his grandfather Enoch. Enoch apparently told Noah's father that the guardians of the sky, or Angels had impregnated his wife and he should go home and raise him as his own. It states that Noah's bloodline is pure which is why he was chosen to repopulate the Earth.

This finding has led scholars to believe that perhaps the Bible if it is based in facts, doesn't tell the whole story. If Noah and his family did truly repopulate the Earth, this may be a description of how we enter the next stages of our evolution. The ark itself may have been something else entirely changed into a story that would have been easier to understand.

To try and give some credibility of what we see as a flying saucer actually traversing the Universe(s), look at what we know. Arguably the fastest physical objects in our solar system is none other than our planets. The simplest way to explain their great speed without crediting their immense size, they are rotating remarkably fast and are possibly propelled by their own gravitational force. Given the descriptions of the capabilities of Alien kind, we have seen they seemingly have mastered this knowledge and have used it to benefit them. They have aircraft is known to rotate very fast, and some sightings throughout time suggest they have the ability of levitation.

Are we capable of mastering these techniques?

Considering the fact they would have a vast knowledge of the Universe(s), given they are capable of traveling between planets, it would be safe to assume they would have an advanced knowledge of Gene technology. This would suggest they would be able to take place in the process we have come to know as Evolution. If this is true, would this mean Evolution isn't a force that happens in nature as we have come to believe, but nothing more than an experimental procedure by a foreign species?

Given the evidence supporting Evolution and the belief everything started out as single cell organisms and slowly evolved into more complex creatures is a completely valid argument. You could argue if they truly had a hand, why did it take so long to achieve our current state?

I can't claim I'm an expert in the field of genetics and all it entails, but what if even given their technology, you just can't jump forward and skip a step because perhaps the process still takes time to weed out abnormalities.

I suppose simply put, you can't jump from a single cell organism to a homo-sapien, because the genetic make-up just couldn't support this drastic transition.

If you were to look at it from this possibility, that would pose possibly and even bigger question. If Evolution as we know it, is not a random occurrence in nature, how did they achieve such a high level of intelligence?

This may in fact cause my theory to collapse on itself. If evolution truly does not exist in Nature that would either suggest they had already formed as intelligence beings in their first stage, or there may indeed be some form a divine intervention that exceed these beings.

What if the truth goes all the way back to the common ancestor we are believed to share with apes. Could this break from our common ancestor be the starting-point of their influence and Evolution as we believe does happen in nature? Would possession of this ability truly make you "God-like?"

In a Scientific standpoint, would the old stories of Angels and Demons not make more sense if they were in fact, Aliens? Would it stand to reason that perhaps there may even in fact be more than one species of alien life? What if the Angels as we have come to known are protecting us from a hostile force that wants to take over Earth? Could this be the great battle the ancient Indian texts described?

If Krishna, Jesus, Muhammad, and Noah were all truly in contact with extraterrestrial being, three of which may have been what we know as Nephilim.. What would that mean for me?

CHAPTER 10: THE END

This has been quite the journey. Many of you may be wondering what I am trying to accomplish. To be completely honest, I'm not entirely sure. At first I genuinely had the idea of uniting everyone together. For too long we have been separated from one another for difference of beliefs. Out of these beliefs war, racism, greed, homo-phobia have all been given credibility. We are better than this. Whichever side you are on, if your beliefs truly make you feel bringing harm to another living creature is in anyway acceptable be it a survival of the fittest viewpoint, or you truly believe you have been given a divine right to claim something that doesn't belong to by any means necessary, well you are part of the problem in our society.

If you have made it this far, I can only assume that you do have the common understanding we need to change. I know this book as the potential of causing great conflict among all groups of people, especially if I am to claim the title of the False Prophet.

Does this make me insane?

I suppose the best way to end this tale would be tell you about who I am and how I ended up where I am today.

I was born dead seven months pre-mature. You may think I should thank that God that I survived but personally I thank the doctors that brought me back to life.

I spent the first few months of my life in an incubator and the doctors ran tests on me to see if I was healthy. They discovered I had a Bicuspid Aorta in my heart. This basically means one of the valves in my heart doesn't close completely and essentially my heart has to work harder than normal. This limits me from anything that might cause me to over exert myself or puts me in danger of taking a blow to the chest such as contact sports.

It should go without saying I was an easy target for bullying. I remember once I had told my parents I was being picked on and asked for permission to fight them, or something along those lines, simply because I didn't want to be punished. They sat me down and told me if I got in a fight and got hit in the chest hard enough I could possibly die.

I was probably anywhere from six to eight years old so needless to say I was scared. From then on I was forced to endure the bullies. I spent a lot of time inside my head which made me socially awkward.

My parents split up many times so my three sisters and I spent most of our childhood moving place to place. We would stay at friends of my moms, we even spent some time in a women and children's shelter. Perhaps one of the most difficult time during this period was when we stayed with my mom's brother.

We all had to share a room that could barely fit us and our belongings. We slept on the floor on beds made out of blankets. This was during the summer where temperatures ranged anywhere from 90 to 108 degrees Fahrenheit with nothing more than a fan to cool us. Luckily our neighbors were kind enough to let us visit whenever we wanted.

I can remember my eight grade year more vividly than others because it was by far my worst and also my greatest year. At the beginning, my parents split up for the last time until they finally divorced. We moved to a pretty bad neighborhood where drugs and overall a bad set of characters lived.

My sisters and I began to rebel against our mother which seems to be what most kids in our position do. We did and said things to each other that still bring me shame. We would skip school or not go all together. For me, it was to escape the bullies not to mention I somehow only had one outfit I could wear. All my clothes had disappeared and all I was left with were the clothes on my back. This made going to school this much harder.

Depression and suicide weighed heavily on my mind.

Towards the end the year we moved in with our cousins. My cousins are the closet things to brothers I've ever had and they allowed me to wear their clothes seeing as I had none. Then for the first time I actually fit in at school.

My life stayed on this path for the remainder of my school years, but then a new problem arose. I started hanging around, well, bad influences. I began taking drugs when I was 15, which for someone with a bad heart, was not a smart decision.

I was fine for the first few years but when I was 17, I ended up in the hospital for severe chest pains. That night is when this began.

This kind of makes me a sap, but when I was lying in the hospital bed the thing that I regretted more than anything was not letting myself getting close to anyone. It's funny out of everything that should've been thinking of, that was the one thing on my mind. I spent my life thinking I wouldn't live long enough to accomplish anything so I held myself back.

That following month was possibly the hardest period of my life. I would wake up feeling like that day would be my last, and go to sleep thinking I wouldn't wake up. I had many nightmares about having heart attacks, wake up with my heart racing, and more chest pains. All I could do was wait for them to pass and fall back asleep.

They say a near death experience changes your outlook of life and I can vouch for this. I let go of my past and understood that someone out there had it far worse than me. I suppose this is when I developed my desire to try and fix the world. I've made many mistakes in my life but I still only have that one regret.

I ignored these, enlightenments, I was having and got myself a steady job working in a factory straight out of high school. I had a 401k and I was paying off a car. After a couple years of working there, I thought my life was on a right on track.

Then out of nowhere, I had an episode of chest pains. I went into the E.R. and they determined that there was nothing wrong with me so they sent me home. Unfortunately I couldn't bring myself to go into work because my chest still felt sore and at that time I genuinely thought this was going to be the end. One week later I experienced another episode, this one far worse and lasting three hours. Once again, the doctors determined there was nothing wrong with me physically.

Upon research of my own, I determined the best explanation was I was having panic attacks. I still can't explain why they started I can only guess I have high anxiety.

So, bringing us to the present, after those episodes I felt it would be best to put all of this down on paper before I was no longer able to... The most contradicting thing about all of this is a feel I am supposed to.

*Crazy, I know.
Here I am, a 20 year old who considers himself an Atheist, dealing with a messiah complex. Is there a greater contradiction?*

Just so none of this gets misinterpreted I feel I should say this. I was very careful in distinguishing information gathered by many people far more intelligent than I am, from my own attempts to putting together this puzzle. I have come across all of this information during my research in many different books, and documentaries. If the connections frighten you in any way, you're not alone.

Are the Gods we have come to worship truly all powerful entities? Or are they nothing more than that of a sophisticated species we know as "little green men?" Were the Aliens sent here to watch over us and guide us on our way? Could this mean the Fallen Angels written in scriptures truly fell because they did feel we weren't worth the time?

Have I fallen right into the devils plan? Have I taken you with me?

There are so many different pieces missing due to the fact that many documents containing vital information to the past could have been lost or discarded completely.

Where does this leave us? Could these be the answers to unlocking the truth about the Universe(s)? Or are these nothing more than the ramblings of man in his decent into insanity..